Acknowledgements

I praise God that I first received the Holy Spirit over 50 years ago, and was baptised in the Holy Spirit 40 years ago. These have been wonderful years of continual discovery of the riches the Lord imparts to us through this most precious gift of Himself!

I am grateful to all those with whom I have shared fellowship in the Holy Spirit during this time, and for the truths we have learned together. They have been wonderful years.

I am thankful to those who have helped with the production of this book, especially to Mary, David and Cliss. To all at Kingdom Faith who join with me in praying for God to revive His Church in the power of the Holy Spirit. To Paula and those who have worked closely with me in the Spirit. And especially to my wife, Caroline, and our family; we have had the privilege of our family life being mightily blessed by God in the life and power of the Holy Spirit. Thank you, Lord!

Colin Urquhart

TRUE Spirit

Colin Urquhart

Kingdom Faith Resources Ltd.
Roffey Place, Old Crawley Road,
HORSHAM West Sussex, RH12 4RU
Tel: 01293 851543 Fax: 01293 854610
E-mail: resources@kingdomfaith.com
www.kingdomfaith.com

First published in Great Britain in March 2003 by Kingdom Faith

Kingdom Faith Church is a registered charity (no.278746)

ISBN 1-900409-44-5

CONTENTS

1

GOD'S PROMISE

God created man in His own image to have fellowship or communion with Him – to know Him, love Him, share His life and enjoy His Presence. Man's sin marred that image and destroyed this unity. However, God's purposes were not to be thwarted; He had planned how He would restore His people and make it possible for them to have an even closer relationship with Him than they had when first created.

Because of their failure, sin, disobedience and rebellion against Him, the Lord had to demonstrate that there was no way that they could possibly love Him or serve Him faithfully through their own efforts. They could not work their way back into unity with Him. They could do nothing to please Him or deserve His forgiveness and acceptance.

Their rebellion against His authority, called 'The Fall,' had infected man's very nature. Instead of the innocence that God had wanted for mankind, the decision to sin meant that everyone of each successive generation was born with a sinful nature. People had hearts intent on pleasing themselves and doing as they wanted. This sinful nature is called 'the flesh' in Scripture, and causes the

... THE FLESH COUNTS FOR NOTHING AND IS INCAPABLE OF PLEASING GOD!

desire to operate independently of God, without any reference to His will or purpose. **Jesus said that in man's flesh, his natural life, there was nothing good; the flesh counts for nothing and is incapable of pleasing God!**

Throughout the Old Testament period God demonstrated that, even though He gave the people His law and commandments, telling them clearly what He was expecting of them, they still refused to obey. He showed them the benefits that would come through walking with Him in obedience:

> *If you fully obey the LORD your God and carefully follow*
> *all his commands that I give you today, the LORD your God*
> *will set you high above all the nations on earth. All these blessings*
> *will come upon you and accompany you if you obey*
> *the LORD your God. (Deuteronomy 28: 1-2)*

The Lord promised to bless His people in the city and the country. Their families would prosper, their cattle and crops would be abundant. They would defeat their enemies and they would become the envy of other nations.

However, to disobey would bring curse upon them. They would experience defeat by their enemies and would become a people in bondage and under God's judgement!

At times the people were intent on obeying the Lord, and when they did so His good promises were fulfilled. But as soon as they began to prosper, compromise and disobedience would set in and they would begin to depart from His ways. Even though God raised up prophets to warn them of the disastrous consequences of such disobedience, they generally took no notice, choosing to pursue their own ways instead.

They daily experienced the curses that God had wanted them to avoid. He allowed such things to happen not only as a punishment, but to encourage them to return to His ways in faithfulness and righteousness so that, once again, He could bless them.

The problem was this: they found they could not sustain obedience to the Lord because of the nature of their hearts. So God was looking toward the time when He would do an entirely new work in the lives of His people. **He would give them new hearts and cause His own Spirit to come and live within them, thus enabling them to walk in His ways, not in their strength but through the presence of God's power within them. God would do nothing less than come to live in them by giving them His own Spirit to live within them!**

I will give you a new heart and put a new spirit in you;
I will remove from you your heart of stone and give you a heart
of flesh. And I will put my Spirit in you and move you to follow my
decrees and be careful to keep my laws. (Ezekiel 36: 26-27)

When they received His Spirit the people would have an entirely different kind of relationship with God. Instead of His laws being written in a book or on tablets of stone, they would be written on their hearts and minds. He would establish a new covenant with them, an agreement in which the promises of the blessings they would receive would far outweigh the promises of the former covenant:

> *"This is the covenant I will make with the house of Israel*
> *after that time," declares the LORD. "I will put my law in their*
> *minds and write it on their hearts. I will be their God,*
> *and they will be my people." (Jeremiah 31: 33)*

The prophet, Joel, described what God would do when He gave His own Spirit to His people.

> *I will pour out my Spirit on all people. Your sons and*
> *daughters will prophesy, your old men will dream dreams,*
> *your young men will see visions. Even on my servants, both men*
> *and women, I will pour out my Spirit in those days.*
> *(Joel 2: 28-29)*

This great gift of receiving God's own Spirit meant His Person, His Presence, His power would be given to young or old, male or female – all who turned to Him with repentance and faith.

This great event could not take place until men and women received God's forgiveness for all their former sins of rebellion and disobedience. The old sinful nature would then be replaced by an entirely new nature. To secure their reconciliation to Him, God sent His Son to take all mankind's sin on Himself, all failure and every negative thing that had affected the people as the consequence of 'The Fall.' Man could not make himself right before God; so God's own Son would come and share our humanity, live in perfect righteousness and obedience to His Father's will, and then offer His life as a perfect sacrifice on behalf of all sinners. By faith in Him and what He did on the cross, they could then receive forgiveness, be justified or made righteous and acceptable in God's sight, and receive a new nature, with God's own Spirit living in them. Paul explains:

> But now a righteousness from God, apart from law, has been made known, to which the Law and the Prophets testify. This righteousness from God comes through faith in Jesus Christ to all who believe. There is no difference, for all have sinned and fall short of the glory of God, and are justified freely by his grace through the redemption that came by Christ Jesus. (Romans 3: 21–24)

Having accomplished all He was sent to do as our Saviour, Jesus returned to heaven. **Then the Holy Spirit, the Spirit who lived in Him, could be poured into the lives of all who believed in Him.** The prophet Isaiah describes the nature of this Spirit:

> The Spirit of the LORD will rest on him – the Spirit of wisdom and of understanding, the Spirit of counsel and power, the Spirit of knowledge and of the fear of the LORD – and he will delight in the fear of the LORD. (Isaiah 11: 2-3)

This is the precious gift that would be given to all who were 'born again' as a result of turning their lives over to Jesus to be their Saviour and Lord. Before we see how we can receive the Holy Spirit, we will look at how He operated in Jesus Himself during His humanity.

2

THE HOLY SPIRIT IN JESUS' MINISTRY

For about thirty years Jesus lived in obscurity. During this time He did not perform any public ministry. He preached no sermons (as far as we know). He did not heal the sick, cast out demons, raise the dead or work any other kind of miracle. He awaited His Father's timing when the Holy Spirit would come upon Him to enable His ministry.

The Holy Spirit is the Spirit of God. He is divine, the third person of the Holy Trinity. He was active in creation and is now the Presence of God at work within creation.

Jesus was conceived by the Holy Spirit. He was the seed placed within Mary's womb as a virgin. During His humanity Jesus had a divine nature and a human mother.

This is how the birth of Jesus Christ came about:
His mother Mary was pledged to be married to Joseph,
but before they came together, she was found to be with child through
the Holy Spirit. (Matthew 1: 18)

A born again person does not find it difficult to believe that Jesus was conceived in this way. When the Holy Spirit gives new life to the believer, the Person of God comes to live within him or her. A new life has been birthed in the believer!

Obviously this is different from the conception of Jesus; and yet the principle is simple, the seed of the Holy Spirit coming to live in the new believer giving him or her a new birth!

Luke describes the visitation Mary received from the angel, Gabriel, telling her of the birth of Jesus:

"Do not be afraid, Mary, you have found favour with God.
You will be with child and give birth to a son, and you are to give
him the name Jesus. He will be great and will be called
the Son of the Most High." (Luke 1: 30-32)

We know little of Jesus' early life, except that *"he was filled with wisdom," (Luke 2: 40)* one of the qualities of the Holy Spirit. Having been conceived by the Holy Spirit and having a divine nature, the Spirit would have been operating in some way in Jesus' life. Yet it was not until He went to the River Jordan to be baptised by John that He received the anointing, the empowering of the Holy Spirit for His ministry.

John the Baptist had been commissioned by God to prepare the way for the ministry of His Son. There had been a prophetic silence over the nation for four hundred years. That silence was broken by this man calling the people to repentance. All Jerusalem and Judea went to hear him and clearly the spiritual "atmosphere" was changing ready for Jesus' ministry.

Jesus insisted that John should baptise Him, not that Jesus had any sin of which to repent, but because He was identifying completely with those He had come to save. John had prophesied of Jesus by saying:

> *"I baptise you with water for repentance. But after me will come one who is more powerful than I, whose sandals I am not fit to carry. He will baptise you with the Holy Spirit and with fire." (Matthew 3: 11)*

The Saviour would be the One who baptised people with God's Spirit. To baptise is to "submerge," or to "infuse completely with." Through Jesus, people would be submerged not only with water for the forgiveness of their sins, but with the life and power of the Holy Spirit. God's Spirit would completely infuse their lives when they received the baptism in the Holy Spirit.

Before this was possible, Jesus would have to fulfil His ministry on earth; and for this, His Father in heaven completely infused *Him* with the Holy Spirit.

It is important to understand that Jesus did not receive the Holy Spirit in this way while He was in the water being baptised by John. The Baptist makes it clear that there is a distinction between water baptism and being baptised in the Holy Spirit. The narrative makes it clear that, *"As soon as Jesus was baptised, he went up out of the water." (Matthew 3: 16)* Luke tells us:

> *As he was praying, heaven was opened and the Holy Spirit descended on him in bodily form like a dove. And a voice came from heaven: "You are my Son, whom I love; with you I am well pleased." (Luke 3: 21-22)*

The angel had revealed that the child to be born was to be called Jesus, which means Saviour. When His ministry begins He becomes the Christ, the Messiah, the Anointed One, not that He was recognised as such immediately.

God acknowledged Him as His Son. Why should God say He was well pleased with Him? Perhaps because He had waited patiently and obediently until this time of anointing before beginning His ministry. Having the heart of love and compassion, He must have wanted to reach out to people in their need, but He waited until the Father's appointed time.

Jesus, full of the Holy Spirit, returned from the Jordan
and was led by the Spirit in the desert, where for forty days
he was tempted by the devil. (Luke 4: 1-2)

This seems a strange way for Jesus' ministry "in the Spirit" to begin. Why should the Spirit lead Him in this way? When He began His ministry in Galilee, Jesus quoted a prophecy from Isaiah:

"The Spirit of the Lord is on me, because he has
anointed me to preach good news to the poor. He has sent
me to proclaim freedom for the prisoners and recovery of sight
for the blind, to release the oppressed, to proclaim the year
of the Lord's favour." (Luke 4: 18-19)

Jesus clearly understood that He was anointed to reach others with the gospel of God's Kingdom. He would fulfil this purpose both in the things He said and did. **Throughout His ministry He made it clear that He remained submitted to the Father in all He did.**

He spoke no words of His own; only those His Father gave Him to speak. He did nothing independently of His Father; only those things He saw the Father doing. He said:

> *"For I have come down from heaven*
> *not to do my will but to do the will of him*
> *who sent me." (John 6: 38)*

This was His "food" – *"to do the will of him who sent me and to finish his work." (John 4: 34)*

What was the substance of Satan's temptations? That Jesus should use the anointing of the Holy Spirit, not to do the will of His Father, but to act independently from the Father; not to use the anointing for the benefit of others, but for His own ends and His own needs.

THROUGHOUT HIS MINISTRY HE MADE IT CLEAR THAT HE REMAINED SUBMITTED TO THE FATHER IN ALL HE DID.

After fasting for forty days Jesus is hungry. The devil suggests to Him that He should use the power available to Him to turn stones into bread. Surely such an act would verify that He is the Son of God! Jesus answered:

> *"It is written: 'Man does not live on bread alone,*
> *but on every word that comes from the mouth of God.'"*
> *(Matthew 4: 4)*

Jesus would not use His anointing at the devil's prompting, but only in obedience to His Father. Neither would He use His power to satisfy Himself in this way; **the anointing of the Holy Spirit was to enable His ministry to others.**

There is an important object lesson for all believers here. God wants to anoint all His children with the life and power of the Holy Spirit. He wants them to be guided by the Spirit as to how to use that anointing. It has not been given for their own selfish ends or enjoyment, but to enable them to bear fruit by being effective in ministry to others. There is to be purity in our motives when using the great resources that are made available to us through the Holy Spirit.

The devil then suggested to Jesus that He should do something spectacular to draw attention to Himself. Finally the enemy offered Jesus the kingdoms of this world if He would only bow down and worship him.

Jesus counteracted both these temptations from scripture. He was to obey His Father, not put Him to the test! When offered power by the devil, He answered:

> *"Away from me, Satan! For it is written: 'Worship the Lord your God, and serve him only.'" (Matthew 4: 10)*

So the purpose of the anointing is to serve God, to live for His glory. Not to do spectacular things to draw attention to self, but use the anointing in obedience to God – for His purposes. **The anointing is not given for people to build a power base for themselves, but to love and serve the Lord, by loving and serving His people.** All this we see outworked in Jesus' ministry.

Jesus spoke very little about the Holy Spirit before the Last Supper, when He taught His disciples about the gift they would receive after His crucifixion, resurrection and return to heaven.

The Holy Spirit is the Spirit of Christ, the Spirit that operated in Him throughout His ministry. He did everything in the power of the Spirit, releasing the supernatural power of God into one natural situation after another. Every healing Jesus performed was a supernatural work of the Spirit. Every time He delivered people from bondage to demonic spirits, the power and authority of the Spirit was being exercised over them through Him. He raised the dead and performed many miracles, each demonstrating the presence of God's Kingdom, each verifying His preaching about the Kingdom. For God's Kingdom is not a matter of talk but of power, Paul tells us. **The presence of that Kingdom is demonstrated whenever God's rule and reign is manifested over sin, the principalities of this world and the power of the devil, in the power of the Holy Spirit.**

When Jesus healed the sick, Matthew explains that He was fulfilling Isaiah's prophecy: *"Here is my servant whom I have chosen, the one I love, in whom I delight; I will put my Spirit on him."* *(Matthew 12: 18)* And Jesus Himself said:

> *"But if I drive out demons by the Spirit of God then the kingdom of God has come upon you." (Matthew 12: 28)*

He put the focus on the Kingdom of God in all He said and did. He wanted the people to turn to God and receive the Kingdom. If they were to seek first the Kingdom of God and His righteousness, everything else would then be added to them. (Matthew 6: 33) **In due course God would empower them with the Holy Spirit to enable them to live as the children of His heavenly Kingdom here on earth!**

Jesus sent His disciples to do the same things as He did, although at that time they were not filled with the Holy Spirit. Clearly they went out with the power of the Holy Spirit, otherwise they would not have been able to return to Jesus with glowing reports of the fruit produced through their ministries. Even the demons submitted to their exercise of authority in His name.

The fact that Jesus did nothing in independence shows how He relied totally on the Father, and would not use the anointing given Him by the Father unless clearly shown by Him what He was to do. Whenever He taught the people they were amazed at the authority with which He taught, another evidence of the Holy Spirit's anointing! And He was full of the joy of the Holy Spirit (see Luke 10: 21). The writer to Hebrews quotes from Psalm 45, when speaking of Jesus.

> *You have loved righteousness and hated wickedness;*
> *therefore God, your God, has set you above your companions by*
> *anointing you with the oil of joy. (Hebrews 1: 9)*

The joy of the Holy Spirit marked Jesus off from all others around Him. And, of course, He was the embodiment of love, which is the first fruit of the Holy Spirit!

3

JESUS' TEACHING ABOUT THE HOLY SPIRIT

Jesus not only taught and acted in the power of the Holy Spirit, He was preparing the way for all who believed in Him to receive this precious gift from God. There was no way in which anyone could *deserve* to have God come and live in him; neither could a person *earn the right* for this to happen. The Holy Spirit was to come as a gift to those who were thirsty for God's power in their lives.

> *Jesus stood and said in a loud voice, "If anyone is thirsty, let him come to me and drink. Whoever believes in me, as the scripture has said, streams of living water will flow from within him." (John 7: 37)*

Jesus implies that it is easy to receive this gift. If you are thirsty for God, you only have to ask. The gift is not given solely for the benefit of the believer, but so that rivers of living water may flow out of him, literally, out of the deep, innermost part of his being. John explains:

> *By this he meant the Spirit, whom those who believed in him*

were later to receive. Up to that time the Spirit had not been
given, since Jesus had not yet been glorified. (John 7: 39)

This explains why Jesus spoke sparingly about the Holy Spirit.
There was little point in doing so until it was possible to receive
Him. He simply holds out the assurance before the people that
God was certainly going to honour the promises concerning the
Holy Spirit. When the time came for them to receive, they would
do so by asking for this wonderful gift.

"Ask, and it will be given you; seek and you will find; knock
and the door will be opened to you. For everyone who asks receives;
he who seeks finds: and to him who knocks, the door will
be opened." (Luke 11: 9)

This is not to ask or seek in a casual manner, but with a
determined, persistent attitude; and yet with the full assurance that
the Father would surely give His Spirit in response to such prayer.

If you then, though you are evil, know how to give good gifts
to your children, how much more will your Father in heaven give
the Holy Spirit to those who ask him! (Luke 11: 13)

Jesus makes it clear that this gift of the Holy Spirit, being God, is
to be reverenced and honoured, never spoken against. Anyone
speaking against Jesus would be forgiven, *"but anyone who speaks*
against the Holy Spirit will not be forgiven, either in this age or in the
age to come." (Matthew 12: 32)

Why should Jesus be so emphatic that to speak against the Holy
Spirit was such a grievous sin? He had been sent by the Father, not

only with the message and power of the Kingdom, but that God's people would be able to be born again and become part of that Kingdom. **There is no way that anyone can become part of that Kingdom without being born of the Spirit.** Jesus said clearly:

> *"I tell you the truth, no one can see the kingdom of God unless he is born again." (John 3: 3)*

THERE IS NO WAY THAT ANYONE CAN BECOME PART OF THAT KINGDOM WITHOUT BEING BORN OF THE SPIRIT.

The phrase translated, "I tell you the truth" is one of great emphasis. Everything Jesus said was true. He used this phrase when He knew people would naturally question what He was about to say, find it difficult to believe or want to avoid the implications of the revelation He was bringing.

Jesus was talking to a Pharisee, named Nicodemus, when He said this. Nicodemus was perplexed and asked Jesus what He meant:

> *"I tell you the truth, no one can enter the kingdom of God unless he is born of water and the Spirit. Flesh gives birth to flesh, but the Spirit gives birth to spirit. You should not be surprised at my saying, 'You must be born again.'" (John 3: 5-7)*

There are a number of important truths to glean from those few verses.

• To be 'born again' can also be literally translated to be 'born from above.' This refers to being born by God, through His Spirit; a definite supernatural event!

- This was the *only* way to become part of God's Kingdom.

- To be 'born of water' could refer to the natural or physical birth as a baby; or it could possibly refer to water baptism.

- You must have not only a natural birth, but a second birth, a supernatural birth by the Holy Spirit.

- Natural men can only give birth to natural men. In other words our natural birth cannot give us entrance into God's Kingdom. There has to be a second birth by the Holy Spirit in response to each individual's repentance and faith. (see Mark 1: 15)

- The human spirit (indicated in the text by a small 's') is spiritually dead until brought alive by the second birth through the Holy Spirit.

The new birth from above causes a person to come alive spiritually, enables him to come into a personal relationship with God and be blessed with all the riches of God's Kingdom. Until then his human spirit lay dormant until brought to life by the Holy Spirit at the second birth. Before his new birth he may have been religious, believed in God, attended church and sought God in prayer. When the Spirit fills him with God's life and power, all these activities immediately come to life in a totally unexpectedly way; for now the believer *knows* the One he worships and to whom he prays! He knows the Lord personally and that he is totally forgiven and accepted by God.

This event is a life-transforming event for most, especially for those who formerly were not religious, had nothing to do with God and may even have doubted His existence! It can be a dramatic event for very religious people such as Saul of Tarsus. For three days he was made blind to show him how blind he had been in resisting

God, refusing to accept Jesus as the Son of God, and even persecuting the Church, believing he was doing God's will in the process.

Though he had been resisting the work of the Holy Spirit in the early Church, he was not guilty of speaking against the Holy Spirit himself. To be ignorant or deceived, as Saul was, is different from cursing the Holy Spirit. If Saul had been guilty of an eternal sin, God would not have made him Paul, the great apostle, who wrote about one third of the New Testament!

THE LAST SUPPER

Jesus used the final evening with His disciples before His crucifixion to explain many highly significant things to them. Here we must limit our concentration to His statements about the Holy Spirit. With His imminent death, resurrection and ascension to heaven, this was the right time to explain the ministry of the Spirit in their lives.

Jesus promises that when He returns to heaven, He will ask His Father to give them His Holy Spirit, the Counsellor, who will be with them forever. Jesus was described in Isaiah's prophecy as the Wonderful Counsellor! The Holy Spirit is "another Counsellor" who will remain with them, and will continue the ministry of the "the Wonderful Counsellor" in and through them after Jesus has returned to heaven.

If you love me, you will obey what I command. And I will ask the Father, and he will give you another Counsellor to be with you forever – the Spirit of truth. (John 14: 15-17)

There is to be a continuity of ministry; the other Counsellor will continue the ministry of the Wonderful Counsellor here on earth – not through the humanity of Jesus that is about to end, but through His Body, the Church. For the Holy Spirit will come not only on those meeting with Jesus at the Last Supper, but on all who subsequently would come to believe in Him.

Jesus is the Truth (John 14: 6); He *"came from the Father, full of grace and truth." (John 1: 14)* He spoke the words of eternal truth and His Spirit is the Spirit of truth, the Counsellor, the Advocate, who will speak to us and for us. And He will speak the eternal truths that Jesus came to proclaim. He explains:

> *"The world cannot accept him, because it neither sees him nor knows him. But you know him, for he lives with you and will be in you." (John 14: 17)*

Here Jesus clearly identifies the Holy Spirit as being His own Spirit, the Spirit that indwelt Him, the Spirit of Christ. Because the world did not accept Jesus, or understand that all He was doing was in the power of the Holy Spirit, therefore the world cannot accept or receive the Holy Spirit. **Those who accept and believe in Jesus are able to receive the Holy Spirit. And when they do so, He will live *in* them, not simply *with* them, as was the case during Jesus' humanity.**

By contrast, those who reject Jesus as Son of God, either then or now, are unable to receive the precious gift of the Holy Spirit. He will not come to live in anyone who rejects the Lordship of Jesus Christ over his or her life.

Because He is the Spirit of truth, the principal ministry or work of the Holy Spirit in the lives of believers will be to keep the truth of what Jesus has said always before them, and to enable them to walk in that truth.

"But the Counsellor, the Holy Spirit, whom the Father will send in my name, will teach you all things, and will remind you of everything I have said to you." (John 14: 26)

This reinforces that those who reject Jesus cannot receive the Holy Spirit, for the Father will send Him in the name of Jesus to all who place their lives under the power and authority of that name. The Holy Spirit will be the disciples' teacher, continuing the role Jesus had played in their lives as their "Rabbi" and Master. The Holy Spirit does *not* want to initiate new teaching, but to remind believers of all that Jesus has said.

HE DOES NOT WANT TO GLORIFY HIMSELF OR DRAW ATTENTION TO HIMSELF.

This points us to a key truth about the Holy Spirit. **He does not want to glorify Himself or draw attention to Himself. He causes the believer to focus on Jesus, what He has said and done. He wants to glorify Jesus.** This is in line with Jesus' attitude to the Father while He fulfilled His earthly ministry. Everything He said and did was to glorify the Father, in obedience to Him, fulfilling the task the Father sent Him to accomplish.

The Holy Spirit "will teach you all things." This is a warning not to accept any teaching that does not come from the Holy Spirit. How is it possible to tell whether teaching we hear comes from God's Spirit, or some false, deceiving spirit?

*"When the Counsellor comes, whom I will send to you
from the Father, the Spirit of truth who goes out from the Father,
he will testify about me." (John 15: 26)*

What is truly of the Holy Spirit will always testify about Jesus, who
is *"the same yesterday, today and forever." (Hebrews 13: 8)* So we need
to beware of anyone who claims to have a fresh revelation of truth
that does not line up exactly with what Jesus has already said!

ANY TRUE REVELATION OF THE HOLY SPIRIT WILL ALWAYS FOCUS ON THE PERSON OF JESUS, THAT WE MIGHT KNOW, LOVE AND SERVE HIM FULLY!

Deceiving spirits can only deceive because
what they say sounds like the truth, but isn't;
it appears to be right but does not come
from God. If a thing is obviously wrong it
will be immediately rejected by those who
know the Truth. The devil is the "deceiver of
the brethren" and can appear as an "angel of
light" because he feeds people with a mixture
of some truth and deception, in an attempt
to throw them offcourse. Unfortunately he is
often too easily successful with fallible
believers, who do not hold steadfastly to the
revelation of God's Word. The devil often appeals to reason or
human understanding; the Holy Spirit keeps us in the revelation of
the Truth, of Jesus, of all He has said and done.

**So any true revelation of the Holy Spirit will always focus on
the Person of Jesus, that we might know, love and serve Him
fully!** The believer, filled with the Holy Spirit, has God in him –
to keep him walking and living in the truth, so he can be an
effective witness to the truth.

*"But I tell you the truth: It is for your good that I am
going away. Unless I go away, the Counsellor will not come to
you; but if I go, I will send him to you." (John 16: 7)*

Jesus does not want to leave the disciples as orphans; He wants to
be closer to them than before; not only *with* them, but in them!
Paul says that the secret of the Christian life is to know that Christ
lives *in* you, only possible because you have received the Holy
Spirit.

THE HOLY SPIRIT IN THE WORLD

Without the Holy Spirit you could not even have become a
Christian! Jesus explains what the ministry of the Holy Spirit will
be in the world, as distinct to His work in believers.

*"When he comes, he will convict the world of guilt
in regard to sin and righteousness and judgement: in regard to
sin, because men do not believe in me; in regard to righteousness,
because I am going to the Father, where you can see me no longer;
and in regard to judgement, because the prince of this world
now stands condemned. (John 16: 8-11)*

The Holy Spirit brings conviction, not condemnation. The devil
wants to condemn by making you feel judged and by causing you
to think that you are beyond hope with no way out of your
dilemmas and problems. The Holy Spirit is very different. He has
no desire to condemn. When He convicts, He points out a person's
sin and failure, but He does not *accuse* Him. **He shows the person
His need of Jesus, points Him to Jesus and the victory of the**

cross, so he may receive forgiveness, acceptance, love and freedom from God.

Before a person is born again the Holy Spirit convicts him of his sins and shows him his need of forgiveness. When convicted he feels guilty, but the Spirit then points to the finished work of Jesus through which he can be set free from his guilt. There is *no* condemnation for those who belong to Christ. And this is what the Holy Spirit works to accomplish: **that the unbeliever will come to faith in Jesus, that he will belong to Christ, free from guilt and condemnation, knowing that *all* his sins have been forgiven.**

Of course if a person stands against the revelation of truth he may remain under conviction for some time, knowing he needs to surrender his life to Jesus, but refusing to do so!

The Holy Spirit convicts those who belong to the world, of their sin and their need of God. He shows them their need of righteousness, to be "right" in the eyes of God, to be at peace with Him. He points to Jesus as our Saviour and the Redeemer; the One who gave His righteous life on the cross as the sacrifice offered to God on behalf of all the unrighteous – everywhere! He is the Redeemer, who bore the punishment of death we deserve that we might be free to be made righteous in God's sight through the forgiveness of *all* our sins; free to receive His precious gift of eternal life.

The Holy Spirit points people to the truth that the *only* way to be made righteous in God's sight is by faith in what Jesus has done. We cannot bring ourselves into right standing with God; it has to be the work of His mercy and grace in accepting all Jesus has done for us in pouring out His life for us in love.

The Holy Spirit also convicts the world in regard to judgement. Jesus is our Saviour and Redeemer, but He is also the Judge of the living and dead. The cross not only became the means of forgiveness, acceptance and salvation for all who believe in Jesus; it declared judgement on the devil and all who deny Jesus. They are judged and condemned by their unbelief, by their refusal to accept the way of salvation God has provided. Jesus explained this earlier, when He spoke of God so loving the world that He gave His One and Only Son, so that *"whoever believes in him shall not perish but have eternal life."*

> *For God did not send his Son into the world to condemn the world, but to save the world through him. Whoever believes in him is not condemned, but whoever does not believe stands condemned already because he has not believed in the name of God's one and only Son. (John 3: 17-18)*

God has no desire to condemn or He would not have sent His Son to be the Saviour of the world! All who receive Jesus are saved from the condemnation that all deserve. Those who reject Him have condemned themselves by refusing to accept Jesus as "the Way, the Truth and the Life"!

The Holy Spirit is working in the world to convict unbelievers of their sin, of their need of God and of their need to know Jesus as Saviour and Lord. The Holy Spirit is showing that it is only through Jesus that anyone can be put right with God. The Holy Spirit shows people that Jesus is the only way to be saved from the judgement that will inevitably come because *"the prince of this world now stands condemned." (John 16: 11)*

Those who prefer a worldly lifestyle to that of God's Kingdom, choose to serve "the prince of this world" and will inevitably join him in the condemnation and judgement already pronounced upon him. God does not desire this for anyone; He wills all men to be saved. But He knows they cannot be saved without accepting the saving, redeeming work of Jesus.

You can see the vital role the Holy Spirit has in bringing the saving work of Jesus to sinners who are in such desperate need of God and His saving love!

THE HOLY SPIRIT IN BELIEVERS

Jesus then refers to the work of the Holy Spirit in believers:

> *"But when he, the Spirit of truth comes, he will guide you into all truth. He will not speak on his own; he will speak only what he hears, and he will tell you what is yet to come." (John 16: 13)*

Again Jesus refers to the Holy Spirit as the Spirit of truth. It seems that this is the central point that the disciples need to understand about the Spirit. Jesus does not talk about the power of the Spirit, nor about the gifts or the fruit He will produce in their lives. He wants them to focus on this central truth – that He is the Spirit of truth! Jesus knows that if they are to become the men of faith, authority and power He wants them to be, then the Holy Spirit of truth will combine with the Word of truth to provide a powerful combination in and among them.

Jesus gives us a number of highly significant truths about the Holy Spirit here:

- "He will guide you into all truth." He does not want you to have partial revelation, or concentrate only on the aspects of the truth that appeal to you. **Believers are to live in "the whole counsel of God."**

HE ALWAYS WORKS IN COMPLETE UNITY WITH THE FATHER AND THE SON.

- "He will not speak on his own." The Holy Spirit living within you as a believer will not decide what to speak to you, or the way in which to lead. **He always works in complete unity with the Father and the Son.**

- "He will speak only what he hears." Whatever He says to you will be revelation from heaven, where the Father and the Son rule and reign. They will direct the Spirit as to what to say. **When you hear the voice of the Spirit, therefore, you are to listen to what heaven is saying to you at that time and in that situation.**

- "He will tell you what is yet to come." We must be careful not to try and use the Holy Spirit as some divine "fortune-teller." Divination is demonic according to scripture. It is not for us to try to make the Holy Spirit tell us what is going to happen in the future; the initiative is with God. The Spirit will speak only what He hears. When heaven wants to tell you what lies ahead He will give you the necessary revelation. God may speak promises that you are then to pray into being; or He may warn you of imminent danger or attack from the enemy, so that you will be on your guard.

It is a great temptation to want to know what lies ahead of us, especially when we have important decisions to make. Jesus tells us not to worry about our lives (Matthew 6: 25), nor about tomorrow, *"for each day has enough trouble of its own." (verse 34)* Each day the Holy Spirit will tell us what we need to know if we are sensitive to His voice. **Often our walk of faith involves obeying what He says to us today, without knowing what lies ahead! One thing is certain; when you need to know "what is yet to come," the Holy Spirit will tell you, because this is what Jesus promises.**

"He will bring glory to me by taking what is mine and making it known to you." (John 16: 14)

- "He will bring glory to me." This reinforces what has been said. The Holy Spirit has no desire to glorify Himself. **His intention is to glorify Jesus.**

- "by taking from what is mine." Remember, He does not want to initiate but to reveal Jesus, what He has said and done: the Spirit of Jesus in you revealing what He has already accomplished. **The life of faith is not trying to make God do what you want, but living in the good of what He has done, believing His promises and knowing that He will cause His life to be evidenced in your life as you co-operate with the Holy Spirit who lives in you.**

- "and making it known to you." There are several different ways in which He can do this.

Through the written Word of God in the scriptures, the Holy Spirit causing the truth to come alive in your spirit.

At such times, it seems the Word is being spoken directly and personally to *you*.

By the "voice" of the Spirit when you pray. This is not usually an audible voice, but an impression the Holy Spirit brings upon your mind. All such revelations are to be tested against the Word of God to ensure that this is truly a word from the Holy Spirit, for it is certainly true that not all the thoughts or ideas you have when praying come from the Lord!

Through a book that is explaining the scriptures. You could receive such revelation through reading this book or any book that is speaking the truth of God's Word. Usually such teaching helps us understand what God is saying in His Word of truth.

Through a sermon or teaching session. Again this will be a matter of the Spirit of truth guiding you into the revelation of the truth of scripture. The spirit and life in God's Word is received through preaching and teaching under the anointing of the Holy Spirit, especially when the speaker lives his message. He is not speaking in a theoretical way but is communicating the life of God's Word through the life of the Holy Spirit!

In conversation. Sometimes something said can be the voice of God's Spirit to you at the most unexpected times, but always totally in line with scripture. It may be a word of encouragement or correction, encouraging you to repent. Often it is a word that will build your confidence and trust in God - not flattery, but a word of truth to your heart.

> *"All that belongs to the Father is mine.*
> *That is why I said the Spirit will take from what is mine*
> *and make it known to you." (John 16: 15)*

Jesus concludes this short section about the Holy Spirit with this amazing statement, which shows the complete co-operation between the three Persons of the Trinity of God. He makes it clear that all that belongs to the Father belongs to Jesus; and all that belongs to the Father and Jesus the Holy Spirit wants to make known to *you*. **All! There is nothing He has that He wants to withhold from you. The Holy Spirit lives in you so that all that belongs to the Father and the Son can be *yours!***

Jesus explained that He and the Father will come to those who love Him "and make our home in him." This He does by the Holy Spirit, the wonderful gift of Himself to us!

4

THE POWER OF THE SPIRIT

At the Last Supper, Jesus concentrated on the Holy Spirit as the Counsellor, the Spirit of truth. When He appeared to the disciples in His risen body, before returning to His Father in heaven, He promised:

> *"In a few days you will be baptised with the Holy Spirit."*
> *(Acts 1: 5)*

You will remember that John the Baptist spoke of Jesus as the One who "will baptise you with the Holy Spirit." Jesus is about to begin the fulfilment of that prophetic word. Soon these disciples, together with over one hundred other believers, will be the first to receive this baptism in the Holy Spirit. And Jesus told the disciples what this would mean.

> *"You will receive power when the Holy Spirit comes on you;*
> *and you will be my witnesses in Jerusalem, and in all Judea and*
> *Samaria, and to the ends of the earth." (Acts 1: 8)*

We have seen that the Holy Spirit enabled the continuity of the ministry of Jesus on earth. Jesus was the Wonderful Counsellor;

the Holy Spirit is another Counsellor who will not leave them. Jesus came full of grace and truth; the Holy Spirit is the Spirit of truth. Jesus came demonstrating the presence of God's Kingdom in the power of the Holy Spirit. **This same power is now to be outpoured on these first believers that they may continue this work of the Kingdom in power.** Paul tells us that *"the kingdom of God is not a matter of talk but of power." (1 Corinthians 4: 20)*

Just as Jesus demonstrated this truth in His ministry, so the believers were to demonstrate it in their ministries, through the Holy Spirit living in them and working through them.

This would be the power they needed to proclaim the gospel of the Kingdom and to demonstrate the truth of what they were proclaiming through the supernatural signs and wonders that would follow their preaching. When He appeared to them in His risen body, Jesus had instructed them:

> *"I am going to send you what my Father has promised;*
> *but stay in the city until you have been clothed with power*
> *from on high." (Luke 24: 49)*

This power and the gift promised by the Father is the Holy Spirit. Having seen that He had overcome death, it must have been tempting for the disciples to go through the streets of Jerusalem shouting: "He has risen! He has risen!" All His claims of being sent by the Father, of being the Messiah, the Christ were vindicated, even though the people did not understand why their Messiah should need to be crucified. But Jesus knew the apostles' proclamation and preaching would not be effective until they had received the Holy Spirit. Only the Holy Spirit would convict the people of their sin in rejecting Jesus; only the Holy Spirit could enable the revelation of truth to impact people's hearts, and so encourage them to repent and believe in Jesus. To go out in their own strength would be fruitless, disastrous even. **To go in the power of the Holy Spirit would enable their witness to be effective, not only in reaching their immediate area, but even the ends of the earth!** Mark records the commission He gave the disciples:

> *"And these signs will accompany those who believe:*
> *In my name they will drive out demons; they will speak in*
> *new tongues; they will pick up snakes with their hands;*
> *and when they drink deadly poisons, it will not harm them*
> *at all; they will place their hands on sick people,*
> *and they will get well." (Mark 16: 17-18)*

Some commentators believe these verses to be a later addition of the original gospel of Mark, as they do not appear in the oldest known manuscripts. If this is true, it gives even greater authority to the words of Jesus that the believers would receive power when the Holy Spirit came upon them, and that they would see signs and wonders accompanying their preaching. For clearly these verses reflect the experience of the early Church. They are not only words of promise; they become words of testimony!

Believers were living in the supernatural dimensions of God's power, clearly God's purpose for Christians of every generation. **God Himself is supernatural, the Kingdom of God is supernatural, the gospel is supernatural, the Holy Spirit is supernatural. So wherever the gospel of God's Kingdom is preached in the power and under the anointing of the Holy**

Spirit, we should expect to see the supernatural works of God's power promised by Jesus. After He had ascended into heaven:

Then the disciples went out and preached everywhere,
and the Lord worked with them and confirmed his word
by the signs that accompanied it. (Mark 16: 20)

WE SHOULD EXPECT TO SEE THE SUPERNATURAL WORKS OF GOD'S POWER PROMISED BY JESUS.

Paul did not believe He had fully preached the gospel unless there were visible signs of God's power to confirm what he proclaimed. He makes this clear towards the end of his epistle to the Romans, his most doctrinal epistle! He communicated the gospel, not only in words, but *"by the power of signs and miracles, through the power of the Spirit. So from Jerusalem all the way around to Illyricum, I have fully proclaimed the gospel of Christ." (Romans 15: 19)*

Whoever receives the Holy Spirit receives His power; and it is the power that enables him or her to be a faithful witness and to perform signs and wonders in the name of Jesus. Jesus said: *"These signs will accompany those who believe." (Mark 16: 17)* Even though they have received the Holy Spirit, believers can be robbed of the evidence of His power through unbelief. In just the same way even Jesus, full of God's power, could not do many miracles at Nazareth because of their unbelief.

It is easy to receive the Holy Spirit; Jesus says that it is out of the deep innermost being of *those who believe* that rivers of living water can flow! Faith enables the release of the Holy Spirit's power in believers. Unbelief renders that power ineffective.

No wonder Jesus said: "By your faith it will be done to you!"

Some preachers trust in the anointing of the Holy Spirit to proclaim the Word of truth, but without expecting the supernatural events of God's power that not only are evidence of the truth of what is preached, but meet the needs of God's people. From the earliest experience of the Church we see that the preaching of the Word and the power of the Spirit belong together. In obedience to Jesus, the disciples waited for the power from on high. The promises of Acts 1 were fulfilled, as recorded in the following chapter.

They were gathered together in prayer, having been brought to the place of being "one in heart and mind." It had been ten days since Jesus had returned to heaven, ten days of prayer and preparation for what was about to happen.

Suddenly a sound like the blowing of a violent wind came from heaven and filled the whole house where they were sitting. They saw what seemed to be tongues of fire that separated and came to rest on each of them. All of them were filled with the Holy Spirit and began to speak in other tongues as the Spirit enabled them. (Acts 2: 2-4)

The Church of Jesus Christ was birthed out of this supernatural event. The Holy Spirit came in a supernatural way to give the disciples the supernatural power Jesus had promised for their ministries. The Spirit came as a violent wind, not a gentle breeze. This speaks of the power of His coming. Tongues of fire speak of the refining fire of God's Spirit, cleansing, making them holy, filling their hearts with the fire of God's love.

So great was this event, they could not find adequate words in their own tongues to express their praise of the Lord. The Holy Spirit came to their rescue enabling them to speak in other tongues – a continual flow of praise without having to think what to say.

A crowd gathered and people were amazed to hear all these diverse languages: *"We hear them declaring the wonders of God in our own tongues!" (Acts 2: 11)* Peter explains that this is fulfilling what God has promised through the prophet, Joel. He then preaches Jesus in the power of the Spirit. Having waited for the power from on high, there is conviction among the people. The Holy Spirit is at work in the whole gathering. "Brothers, what shall we do?" they cry out, having been "cut to the heart."

> *"Repent and be baptised, every one of you, in the name of Jesus Christ for the forgiveness of your sins. And you will receive the gift of the Holy Spirit. The promise is for you and your children and for all who are far off – for all whom the Lord our God will call." (Acts 2: 38-39)*

GOD WANTED TO EMPOWER ALL HIS PEOPLE.

That day 3,000 were saved and added to the Church. It had been worth waiting for the Holy Spirit! From the very beginning the disciples knew that the promised gift of the Spirit was for every believer, not just for the apostles or the original friends of Jesus. **God wanted to empower all His people.**

In the exciting days that followed, the corporate life of the Church began to develop. The people devoted themselves to learning God's Word, the Holy Spirit of truth guiding them into all the truth.

They began to share their lives in covenant love for one another. And *"many wonders and miraculous signs were done by the apostles."* (Acts 2: 43)

Already they were seeing the outworking of Jesus' promise that they would do the same things as Jesus did. One of the mighty healings that took place was of the cripple who was carried every day and placed at the Temple gate. Peter said to him:

> *"Silver and gold I do not have, but what I have I give you.*
> *In the name of Jesus Christ of Nazareth, walk." Taking him by*
> *the right hand, he helped him up, and instantly the man's feet and*
> *ankles become strong. He jumped to his feet and began to walk. Then*
> *he went with them into the temple courts, walking and jumping,*
> *and praising God. (Acts 3: 6-8)*

Here was the power of the Holy Spirit operating through the apostle. He knew he had the authority to act in the name of Jesus, and the power of His Spirit to enable the miracle to take place. This healing caused a considerable stir among the people and especially the leaders who had opposed Jesus. Peter had to say to the people: *"Why do you stare at us as if by our own power or godliness we had made this man walk?" (Acts 3: 12)* This was not their own power, but God's Spirit working through the apostles! **The Spirit was enabling them to act in Jesus' name, on His behalf, doing His works, continuing His ministry of healing!**

The apostles were hauled before the Council, but released for everyone had to acknowledge that a mighty work had taken place. On their release they returned to the company of believers. With the increase of opposition they prayed, asking the Lord to *"enable your servants to speak your word with great boldness. Stretch out your hand to heal and perform miraculous signs and wonders through the name of your holy servant Jesus." (Acts 4: 29-30)*

This is an extraordinary prayer, for they had already been speaking with great boldness and a wonderful miracle that had impacted the whole city had taken place. Far from being deterred by opposition, these believers saw their need was for greater boldness and more power to be manifested in miraculous ways. They did not specifically ask for further empowering from the Holy Spirit, but how did God answer their prayer?

> *After they prayed, the place where they were meeting was shaken. And they were all filled with the Holy Spirit and spoke the word of God boldly. (Acts 4: 31)*

God's answer was to fill them all with the Holy Spirit – again! None of them accused God of getting His theology wrong, by saying it was only possible to receive the Holy Spirit once! **Even those who had been filled were filled again.**

Why should God shake the building, for He never does anything without purpose? I believe He was demonstrating that the Spirit was coming upon them again – as He had at Pentecost. This was not simply a stirring of the gift they had already received. I have been in a substantial stone building that has been shaken by the Holy Spirit in this way, and it was an awesome experience. Many wonderful works of power occurred that evening!

So it is possible to receive the Holy Spirit on more than one occasion, as clearly stated in scripture. Not all believers were baptised in the Spirit immediately. Peter and John were sent to Samaria to pray for believers who had been baptised but *"the Holy Spirit had not yet come upon any of them." (Acts 8: 16)* So this receiving of the Holy Spirit was seen as a distinct event from the initial act of repentance and baptism.

There is no space here to continue to speak of the exciting times recorded in the Acts of the Apostles, as the early Church learned how to live in the supernatural empowering of God's Spirit. **But the Holy Spirit is the same Spirit today; He has lost none of His power or gifts. So we should expect to see Him working now as He worked then: in supernatural power, demonstrating the presence of God's Kingdom in and among His people.**

5

THE GIFTS OF THE HOLY SPIRIT

The infilling of the Holy Spirit was for every believer, so God's life and power could be manifested through each one of them. If God's purpose was for the Holy Spirit's authority to be only for those in full-time ministry or in church leadership, the gift would have been confined to such people. No, the gift was for every believer, because **God desired to empower *all* who put their faith in Him.** From the moment of receiving the Holy Spirit, the "gifts" or "manifestations" of the Holy Spirit are available to all who have received His power. The Holy Spirit can manifest His Presence and

GOD DESIRED TO EMPOWER ALL WHO PUT THEIR FAITH IN HIM.

Power in many different ways. Here we will confine ourselves to the gifts (charismata) that Paul lists in 1 Corinthians. These gifts were so readily available to all the believers that they were being mishandled during the public meetings of the Church. Paul wants to correct the abuses and so teaches them:

There are different kinds of gifts, but the same Spirit.
There are different kinds of service, but the same Lord. There are
different kinds of working, but the same God works all
of them in all men. (1 Corinthians 12: 4-6)

The Holy Spirit will manifest Himself and His power through a whole variety of gifts. It is important to realise that these are not different spirits operating but the same Spirit in different ways. So there is to be no competition in the use of gifts.

> *Now to each one the manifestation of the Spirit*
> *is given for the common good. (1 Corinthians 12: 7)*

This is vital to understand. **The demonstration of the gift is not given for the sole benefit of the one manifesting it, and certainly not that he or she may be glorified in any way.** No the gift is for the benefit of *all* who are present.

> *To one there is given through the Spirit the*
> *message of wisdom, to another the message of knowledge*
> *by means of the same Spirit, to another faith by the*
> *same Spirit, to another gifts of healing by that one Spirit,*
> *to another miraculous powers, to another prophecy, to another*
> *distinguishing between spirits, to another speaking in different*
> *kinds of tongues, and to still another the interpretation*
> *of tongues. All these are the work of one and the same Spirit,*
> *and he gives them to each one, just as he determines.*
> *(1 Corinthians 12: 8-11)*

Paul does not mean to imply that a believer can only have one gift of the Spirit. He is writing, remember, to correct the chaos and confusion at Corinth because there gifts were being misused. If you have a gift it is yours to use, but you need to be sensitive to God's leading so that you use the right gift, at the right time, in the right way; not out of selfish interest, but for the common good.

However, although Paul is speaking here about the use of the gifts in public worship, they can be used at other times, whenever the believer needs to use them. We will briefly consider each of these manifestations of the same Holy Spirit.

THE WORD OF WISDOM - The NIV translation "message" is not helpful, for the Greek word is "logos," meaning "word," used for revelation of God's unchanging truth. The word of wisdom is usually the Holy Spirit reminding you of the right scripture at the right time. There are many times when we do not know what to say from our human understanding of a situation. The Holy Spirit will give us a word of wisdom if we ask Him for one. Jesus promised that the Spirit would provide when we do not know what to say. When we need wisdom we only have to ask for it!

THE WORD OF KNOWLEDGE - Again the Greek word is "logos." **This is a word from God to give us knowledge or understanding supernaturally about the situation that confronts us.** Words of knowledge can be given in times of ministry, making us aware of specific things the Spirit is doing or is prepared to do. When these words are spoken in faith, the power of God can come on people spontaneously to heal supernaturally.

When giving counsel, or dealing with a particularly difficult issue, the Spirit can give you a word of knowledge to reveal the true nature of the problem you need to confront. Sometimes the person you are wanting to help is being evasive, or he may not be aware of the nature of the real problem. A word of knowledge can save much time by enabling you to get to the heart of the issue immediately.

FAITH - Faith can be given you by the Holy Spirit. Faith comes from "hearing" God's Word. The Holy Spirit can take a verse of scripture and cause it to become God's voice to you at that moment. This enables faith to rise up within you, for you have heard from God. You know what to believe, what to speak into being with faith.

This is an immense help in particular situations. **But the Holy Spirit also wants to enable us to live a life of consistent faith, whereby we expect God's supernatural enabling and intervention daily.** You see this gift operating in some Christians, who seem to live on a higher level of faith from the norm. Remember, *all* these gifts are available to *all* believers. He can enable you to live in that dynamic of faith if that is what you genuinely want Him to work *in you!*

GIFTS OF HEALINGS - In the Greek both words are in the plural. There are two ways of understanding this gift – and both are true. The gifts are the healings. Paul is not saying that some people have a healing gift; that is an occult claim. Never let anyone pray for you who claims to have such a gift.

No, the gifts (in the plural) are the healings that the Holy Spirit works in the lives of God's people. **It is God who heals through the faith, prayer and ministry of His people.**

We can understand the gifts of healings being the specific healings given to some people. Or we can interpret this as meaning that the Holy Spirit uses some people to impart gifts of healings to many people. He or she has a healing ministry, therefore. However, we must remember that any believer can lay hands on the sick with faith, and they shall recover!

MIRACULOUS POWERS - Because the Church is to live in the supernatural dimension of God's power, we should expect miracles, God's supernatural intervention into the natural order of things. Jesus teaches His disciples (including believers today!) to expect such intervention as being normal. This is the purpose of prayer.

Miracles can be of many different kinds, some small, some great; but all are evidences of the Lord's love, mercy and grace towards us. He is the Lord *"who is able to do immeasurably more than all we ask or imagine, according to his power that is at work within us."* *(Ephesians 3: 20)* And that power is the Holy Spirit.

Some have particular faith for miracles. I know one brother who has seen over 200 raised from the dead in his ministry! But every believer should be open for God's miraculous intervention and provision. He loves to bless His children.

PROPHECY - This is God speaking to His people by His Spirit, either personally or corporately. Some prophecy is predictive, speaking to us of future events; but this accounts for only a very small proportion of true prophecies.

God is much more concerned that we know what He is saying to us NOW, into our present situation. He is the Good Shepherd and His sheep know His voice; and He intends that we should be talking and listening to Him daily.

A verse or passage of scripture can become prophetic when the Holy Spirit speaks it to your heart in such a way that it becomes a NOW word. The Holy Spirit can inspire prophetic words and pictures; but all these are to be tested (not by the one receiving them) to ensure they are authentically from God's Spirit. This must be done in the case of directional words that will affect major decisions in a believer's life. In this case the prophetic word or revelation should be submitted to someone in spiritual authority over the believer.

This is for the Christian's security, to save him or her from making serious mistakes. It is a sign of spiritual insecurity (and usually deception) when a Christian refuses to submit what he has "heard" to others. He is afraid that those over him will not agree, an obvious indication that he does not want to be sure of the truth; he is only concerned that people will agree with him! This opens the door wide to deception. Better to go to those with greater experience of the Holy Spirit who can bear witness that what has been heard is truly from the Spirit of God.

We should not be afraid to listen to the Lord, however. **Paul tells us to** *"eagerly desire spiritual gifts, especially the gift of prophecy." (1 Corinthians 14: 1)* We must learn to detect the voice of the Spirit.

DISTINGUISHING BETWEEN SPIRITS - This is another essential gift for believers, for there are many other spirits at work in society around us, all of them in opposition to the Holy Spirit!

This gift enables us to discover what spirit is operating at any given time. For example, is a person speaking from God when he or she brings a "prophecy"; or is this a soulish word that comes from the person's own understanding of the situation; or is this a word from a deceiving spirit?

No matter what situation you are in, the Holy Spirit can give you the witness when something is not right. You may not be able to see what exactly is wrong with what is said or done; you simply know in your spirit that something is not right. This is beyond the powers of reason; it is a supernatural witness of the Holy Spirit. Experience will teach you to heed such warnings and not ignore them, even if you do not fully understand what is wrong. You will always regret ignoring a warning from the Holy Spirit!

There are other ways in which this gift is used in ministry. For example, when praying for people to be healed, sometimes Jesus took authority over demonic spirits of infirmity that had obviously caused the sickness. At other times He simply spoke a word of authority or faith and the person was healed. So we need to be able to discern when demonic spirits are causing sickness, oppression or some distress in a person's life, or when there are other causes. Without such knowledge it is possible to minister to a person in completely the wrong way, which will only lead to failure and frustration.

When we heed the witness of the Holy Spirit, we can exercise authority in the name of Jesus and experience victory. For He that is in us (the Holy Spirit) is greater than he that is in the world.

SPEAKING IN DIFFERENT KINDS OF TONGUES - This is the most commonly used (and talked about!) gift. It is given to all who have received the Holy Spirit. Not all have necessarily manifested this gift, though. You cannot use what you do not believe you have. Some wait for the manifestation in order to believe they have been filled with the Holy Spirit. They are putting the cart before the horse!

Jesus promises that "all who ask receive," and teaches us to believe that we have received whatever we ask in prayer. Believe that God has been faithful to His promise and has given you His Spirit, if you have asked to be filled. Then understand that you can speak in tongues; the gift is already there waiting to be released through your life. I have known countless numbers of people to experience the release of this gift of speaking in tongues when they have approached the matter with faith in this way.

INTERPRETATION OF TONGUES - The gift of tongues is to be used extensively in the believer's personal prayer life. For he who speaks in a tongue "edifies himself." Intellectual though he was, Paul was thankful that he spoke in tongues more than all those to whom he wrote.

The gift of tongues enables you to pray beyond your understanding. The Holy Spirit within you always knows what to pray. So the Holy Spirit can pray in you and for you. In which case you should also pray for an interpretation; then your understanding will be enlarged. **You will learn something of what the Spirit is praying in and through you.**

However the use of tongues in a public utterance (when all others are quietly listening) is always to be accompanied by a word of interpretation. **In public there must be interpretation, otherwise those present will not understand what has been said.** So Paul teaches that in a public meeting, prophecy is the better gift so that all may readily understand what is said and be edified.

This is not to be confused with the practice of all speaking or singing in the Spirit together. This produces very beautiful harmonies for the glory of God. Many who cannot sing in tune in the natural, can sing beautifully in the Spirit! Even when used corporately in worship there can be a flowing from tongues to the natural, then back to tongues and so on – and you will see that the Holy Spirit is directing the worship to the glory of the Father and the Son. He enables us to worship in spirit and truth. Paul says:

> *I will pray with my spirit, but I will also pray with my mind;*
> *I will sing with my spirit, but I will also sing with my mind.*
> *(1 Corinthians 14: 15)*

6

THE FRUIT OF THE HOLY SPIRIT

All the gifts of the Spirit are available from the moment we have first received the Holy Spirit. Yet there is another, deeper and long-lasting work that God wants to do in every believer: reproducing the character of Jesus in him or her. We are, *"being transformed into his likeness with ever-increasing glory, which comes from the Lord, who is the Spirit."* (2 Corinthians 3: 18)

Paul goes on to explain that *"we have this treasure in jars of clay to show that this all-surpassing power is from God and not from us."* (2 Corinthians 4: 7) **It is important to understand that the power and gifts that come from the Holy Spirit are quite distinct from this work to make us increasingly like Jesus, so that more of His character can be reproduced in us for His glory.**

This process is referred to as the fruit of the Spirit. Gifts are given, fruit grows. Just as the gifts are available to all, so the fruit is to "grow" in all!

But the fruit of the Spirit is love, joy, peace, patience, kindness, goodness, faithfulness, gentleness and self-control. (Galatians 5: 22-23)

When you look at the heart of these qualities you can readily appreciate three things:

- These are the qualities of His life that God wants to reproduce in you as His child, through the work of the Holy Spirit.

- These are the qualities that you want to see increase in your life. We all want to be more loving, joyful, peaceful and patient!

- These are the qualities that all who know you will be very thankful to see increasing in your life!

THE FRUIT WILL GROW ACCORDING TO OUR WILLINGNESS ...

The gifts of the Spirit can only be used by learning to co-operate with the Holy Spirit. He will never force us to use any of them. So also with the fruit of the Spirit; **the fruit will grow according to our willingness to allow the Lord to reproduce these qualities in us, each of them being a characteristic of the life of Christ in us!**

Paul explains that the flesh, your self-life or natural life, is in direct opposition to the life of the Spirit. This is why Jesus says that it is necessary to deny this self-life in order to follow Him. This is not an invitation to fight the flesh life. That accomplishes nothing, except to stir up the very desires that oppose God's purposes in your life. No, the only way to overcome the flesh is to walk in the Spirit.

Live by the Spirit, and you will not gratify the desires of the flesh. [Literal translation] *(Galatians 5: 16)*

The flesh is naturally self-seeking rather than loving, complaining rather than joyful, prone to worry instead of being peaceful, impatient, unkind, unreliable, harsh and lacking self-control. That is the old nature. But God has given a new nature to believers, and the Holy Spirit living within them enables the life of Jesus to grow increasingly and to be expressed through their lives. However, we have to realise that these things go hand in hand: denying the self and encouraging dependence on the Spirit. The Spirit and the flesh do not co-exist easily!

The flesh desires what is contrary to the Spirit, Paul explains, and the Spirit what is contrary to the flesh. *"They are in conflict with each other, so that you do not know what you want."* (Galatians 5: 17) **God gives us the authority and power to withstand the demands and temptations of the flesh, and to allow the life of the Spirit to radiate more fully through us.** It is not a question of trying to be more loving or joyful or peaceful or patient. As we submit ourselves to the Lord and earnestly desire that the Holy Spirit reproduce His life in us, so we shall be glad to see more of Him and less of self being manifested in our lives!

He wants to reproduce these qualities in you. When that is what you want also, and pray to that end, then He will have His way! Not by the might or strength of your own efforts, but by His Spirit.

> *For you were once in darkness, but now you are light in the Lord. Live as children of light (for the fruit of the light consists in all goodness, righteousness and truth) and find out what pleases the Lord. (Ephesians 5: 8-10)*

Earlier Paul had prayed for the Ephesian believers that God *"may strengthen you with power through his Spirit in your inner being, so that Christ may dwell in your hearts through faith."* (Ephesians 3: 16-17) So whether we talk of the gifts of the Spirit or the fruit He wants to reproduce in us, both are the working of His power within us in co-operation with our faith.

God wants you to exercise faith to use the gifts. He wants you to believe Him to reproduce the fruit of the Spirit within you. It is not a matter of saying passively that He will eventually make you more loving, joyful and so on. No, **God wants you to use your faith activity to believe Him to do this, to desire Him to work those things in the deepest part of your being; to co-operate with Him by denying the flesh and choosing to walk daily in the Spirit.**

7

CHARISMA AND CHARACTER

We have seen that the charismatic gifts of the Holy Spirit are available to every believer as soon as he or she has been filled with the Holy Spirit. It is possible to see these gifts operating in the life of someone with obvious character flaws that do not glorify Jesus. This causes some Christians to feel perplexed.

A gift is a gift and cannot be earned by good behaviour! God has chosen to place His Spirit in us as soon as we entrust our lives to Him. He does not wait until we attain some degree of perfection or improvement that proves us worthy to achieve the gift of the Holy Spirit. Such thinking flies directly in the face of the gospel of God's grace.

No matter how "new" a Christian is, the life and power of the Holy Spirit can be manifested immediately in his or her life. I know a believer who, on the first day of his life in the Spirit, raised the dead because he wanted to prove the God in whom He had put His trust!

So we are to exercise the gifts, despite all the things in our lives that do not reflect Jesus or glorify Him! **However, this does not mean**

that we should ignore the character changes the Spirit wants to bring about in us, or to imagine that such changes do not matter. Defects of character can lead to sin, even serious sin. When we grieve the Lord He does not remove the presence of the Spirit from us; He has promised not to do that. Instead, the Holy Spirit will convict us of the sin in order to draw us to repentance, which is not only receiving forgiveness, but turning away from sin. If, when convicted, somebody persists in the sin, refusing to repent and change his lifestyle, then the Lord will allow that serious sin to be exposed. This undermines the use of the gifts, of the anointing on a believer's life.

From time to time, it is sad to hear of a brother or sister in Christ who has fallen into grievous sin of some kind. That believer might be renowned for the mighty way in which God has used him or her. People are confused. "How could God use a person like that, who was guilty of such sin?" they ask. The answer is simple. That believer was using the gifts he or she had received for the benefit of others. God allowed that out of love for those being saved, healed or blessed. At the same time, the sin in that believer's life grieved God.

> IN HIS MERCY, GOD ALWAYS GIVES TIME AND OPPORTUNITY TO REPENT.

In His mercy, God always gives time and opportunity to repent. Refusal to do this leads to public disclosure of the sin, personal shame and humiliation for the believer, ensuring that there has to be a change in lifestyle otherwise those with a love for God's righteous ways will no longer stay interested in that believer's anointing or spiritual gifts! One of the most awesome things Jesus said concerns this matter:

> *"Not everyone who says to me, 'Lord, Lord,' will enter*
> *the kingdom of heaven, but only he who does the will of my*
> *Father who is in heaven. Many will say to me on that day,*
> *'Lord, Lord, did we not prophesy in your name, and in your name*
> *drive out demons and perform many miracles?' Then I will*
> *tell them plainly, 'I never knew you. Away from me,*
> *you evildoers!'" (Matthew 7: 21-23)*

We can fool others and even ourselves by thinking our sinful ways do not matter because we have received the Holy Spirit and are gifted by God; but we cannot fool the Lord. Because His Spirit is in us He not only is aware of all we do, but the motives that lie behind our actions. He knows our every thought, and our words even before we speak them! If we allow sin to go on unconfessed and uncorrected we are not truly living for God's glory, neither are we co-operating fully with the Holy Spirit in bringing about the changes in our characters that He wants to work in us, known as His sanctifying work in us; making us holy, more like Jesus!

From all this we can learn that **God is concerned about the charisma or anointing on our lives; but He is concerned still more with character.** He lives within us in the person of the Holy Spirit that we may live in the good of His power that we might also be the holy people he has called us to be, devoted to fulfilling His will for us both individually and as His Church.

Other titles in this series include:

TRUE AUTHORITY
TRUE CHURCH
TRUE COVENANT
TRUE DISCIPLES
TRUE FAITH
TRUE GOD
TRUE GRACE
TRUE LIFE
TRUE LOVE
TRUE SALVATION
TRUE WORSHIP

All these books by Colin Urquhart and a catalogue of other titles and teaching materials can be obtained from:

Kingdom Faith Resources, Roffey Place, Old Crawley Road Faygate, Horsham, West Sussex RH12 4RU.
Telephone 01293 854 600 email: resources@kingdomfaith.com